20 DAY CHRISTMAS DEVOTIONAL

20 DAY CHRISTMAS DEVOTIONAL

SOMMER AMANDA KELLY

CONTENTS

INTRODUCTION

Thank you for taking time to read this book, my first holiday book! I'm proud to say that this book is my second book I've written for this year 2024! Praise God because He's been so good to me! For those of you who may or may not know my previous book that I wrote was called "Strength For Enduring Adversity" was released late May and early June of 2024. Of course that book was about enduring the hard times of life. For those of you who bought it, read it, and it touched your life or the life of someone else, praise the Lord! For those who haven't gotten it, I'd highly encourage you to get it. About this book, Christmas has always been a special time of the year for me. Enjoying Christmas carols, family traditions, hearing sermons from church, and watching movies about Nativity among other things has been so special to me. We also know that Christmas can be a very busy, stressful, and emotional time of the year. That being said I hope and pray that this 20

Day Christmas Devotional encourages you to remember the reason for the season but also to find joy and fulfillment in the midst of such a crazy time of the year. Sit back, relax, and come with me as we dig deep twenty days as we're about to celebrate the most wonderful time of the year!

DAY 1 THANKING GOD FOR ANOTHER CHRISTMAS SEASON

can remember when I was a kid whether at home or at church, someone would ask me or ask someone what they were thankful for. I remember hearing someone say. "Thank God that He woke us up this morning!" I've also heard someone say. "What a blessing it is to be in the land among the living!" Or if I or someone had a birthday, we'd always express gratitude how we made it another birthday no matter how old we get! What does that mean? Simply put it's a blessing that God allowed us to make another day, week, month, and year! That is definitely something not to take for granted. I know for me what a blessing that is, especially someone who's been through loss (You can read my previous book "Strength For Enduring Adversity" to read about many storms I've been through) especially of loved ones. Any of you who have lost a loved one as well whether it be through murder, car crash, sickness, or miscarriage knows how painful that is but death forces us to remember what's important in life. Since enduring multiple deaths of loved ones I know how blessed I am to make it another day.

I'm not saying that life is easy by any means or that there's no difficulty in our days because as I said, life is hard. But remembering that God will get us through those days is important to remember. I want you all to know and remember that in the midst of the crazy/busy time of Christmas, I want you to pause and thank God you made it another Christmas! Also the Bible says in Psalm 90:12 a Psalm of Moses that says "Teach us to number our days for us to know how few they are. Help us to live them as we should." I know I'm thankful for that because I'm sure we all can think about folks who didn't make it to another Christmas, Thanksgiving, or even New Years! It could be because they're serving in the military, (it's important to pray for our veterans) they could be missionaries overseas, (we need to pray for missionaries overseas) they moved away, (people move far away for various reasons) or simply they passed away. Whatever the reason it is, some people may not be here for the Christmas season but we gotta make it another day and make it another Christmas. Let's pause and be thankful to God we made it another Christmas!

PRAYER

"Dear God I come before You in Jesus name Lord thank you that I got to make it another day and make it another year as we honor the birth of Your Son forgive me Lord for taking my days for granted Forgive me Lord for forgetting to thank you like I should Lord help me make the most of the Christmas season as well as telling others the good news of Your Son coming to the Lord I ask this in Jesus name I pray amen."

SCRIPTURE VERSES

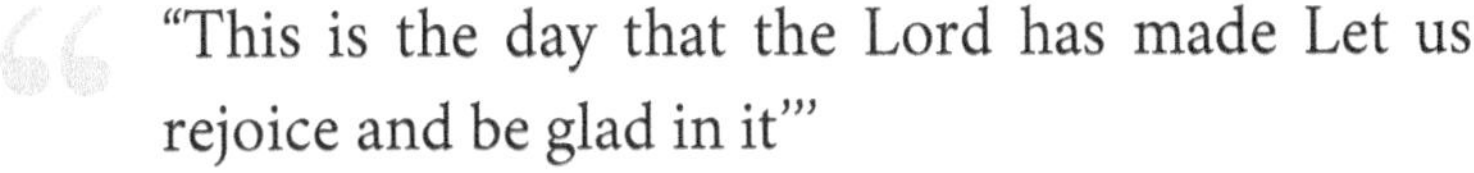

"This is the day that the Lord has made Let us rejoice and be glad in it'"

— PSALM 118:24

"In all things give thanks This is the will of God in Christ Jesus concerning you'"

— 1 THESSALONIANS 5:18

DAY 2 REMEMBERING GOD'S PROMISE TO ADAM AND EVE

I'm sure most of us, especially those who grew up in church, know the story of Adam and Eve. We also know the creation story of how God made the world in six days and you can read all about it in Genesis chapters 1 and 2. We also know that God made Adam which means "man or out of the dust" and breathed life in him and God took Adam's rib and made Eve. Eve's name means "mother of all living." God made Adam and Eve to be one with Him and with one another. God made Adam and Eve to be "one" with Him and to be "one" with each other. The world before the fall was perfect if you can imagine that. Of course we all know the story of the serpent who really was used by the devil to trick Adam and Eve into eating the forbidden fruit with the tree in the middle of the Garden of Eden. That was the only tree God commanded them not to eat but they ate it anyway and from that moment on everything got turned upside down. That's how sin came into the world separating humanity from God, people from each other, animals being a threat to humanity, (especially wild animals) poverty, sickness, death, and so much more.

But in the midst of the fall, God made a promise to Adam and Eve. In fact God promised in Genesis 3:15 that says that God "Put enmity between the serpent and the seed of the woman. His seed and her offspring.He will crush your head and you will bruise his heel." In other words God already had a solution and promised that through Eve's seed a Savior would come that His heel would be bruised by the enemy (the cross of Calvary) and He would crush the enemy's head! Of course we know that to be our Lord and Savior Jesus Christ! Another point I want to make is long before the world was made, Jesus was the Lamb slain before the foundation of the world! Before the world was created our Heavenly Father devised a plan to save us from our sin! Simply put Adam and Eve's sin was not a surprise to God! Am I justifying Adam and Eve's sin? Of course not because sin has consequences but God already had a solution before it all began. Let us be thankful this Christmas season as well as year around for God's promise to Adam and Eve that a Savior came to take away our sins and through us accepting Him was able to put us in right standing with Father God!

PRAYER

"Thank you Heavenly Father for devising a plan for sending Your Son Jesus to save me before the world was and after Adam and Eve sinned I ask You Lord to forgive me of my sins wash me and cleanse me with Your blood Forgive me Lord for taking what Your Son did for granted and help me to ever be so thankful this Christmas season and throughout the year I ask this in Jesus name I pray amen"

SCRIPTURE VERSES

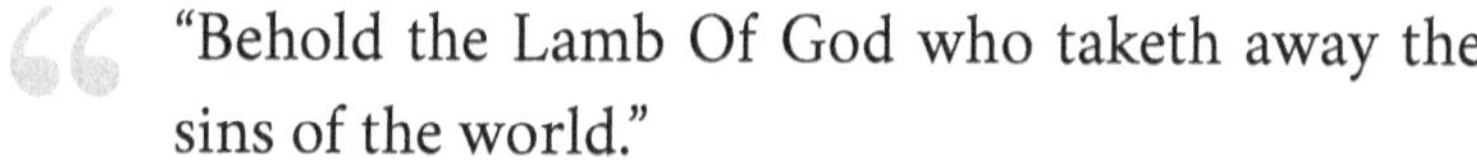

"Behold the Lamb Of God who taketh away the sins of the world."

— JOHN 1:29

"While we were yet sinners Christ died for us"

— ROMANS 5:8

DAY 3 REMEMBERING GOD'S PROMISE THROUGH THE OLD TESTAMENT PROPHETS

*L*et's be honest here. I know that prophecy gets a "bad wrap." Well let me say it like this. I know that many people get skeptical over prophets. Perhaps it could be that a "prophecy was off," a prophet can be arrogant, or one way or another left a person with a "bad taste in their mouth." Regardless of that being the case, the prophetic still is a spiritual gift and it must be used to glorify God. In fact 1 Corinthians 12:1-11 talks about it being one of the gifts of the Spirit and Ephesians 4:11 talks about it being one of the "five-fold ministry gifts." (Apostleship, pastoring, evangelism, and teaching are included too.Also God will deal and judge prophets who get off in His time but we are to pray for them and ourselves.) But that's not the point of this chapter. The point of this chapter is to remember what the Old Testament prophets said concerning the coming of our Lord and Savior Jesus Christ. Here's an important fact to remember. We mentioned in the previous chapter how God made a promise to Adam and Eve, the first man and first woman, after they sinned that a Savior would come through their offspring. Well did you know that God spoke to the Old Testament prophets about His Son's coming 700 years before it happened? Isn't that amazing?

To give you some examples the prophet Isaiah prophesied in Isaiah 7:14 that a virgin would conceive and bear a Son and call His name Emmanuel which means "God is with us." The prophet Isaiah in 9:6,7 says "For unto us a Child is born and unto us a Son is given.The government shall be upon His shoulders and His name shall be called Wonderful Counsellor, The Mighty God, the Everlasting Father, the Prince of Peace." The prophet Micah in Micah 5:2 prophesied where Christ would be born that He would be born in Bethlehem which was a small town is why the famous Christmas carol is called "O Little Town Of Bethlehem." (I'll share more about Christmas carols in another chapter!) These are a few of many prophecies that prophesied Christ's coming and we saw the fulfillment of that 2,000 plus years ago! Let us be thankful to our Heavenly Father for keeping His promises even though it took a long time to happen and that His Son Jesus came. Let's thank and honor our Lord for speaking through prophets (He still speaks through prophets today) and Christ fulfilled those promises during His first coming and will fulfill the rest of them at His Second coming!

PRAYER

"Dear God thank you that You spoke through the prophets in the Old Testaments and that You speak through prophets today Thank you Lord for fulfilling the prophecies at Your First coming knowing that You'll fulfill prophecies of Your Second Coming as well About prophets of today Lord help them be humble, biblical, and speak led by Your Spirit as the Old Testament prophets did Let prophets of today not have 'their own agenda' but Your agenda I ask this in Jesus name I pray amen."

SCRIPTURE VERSES

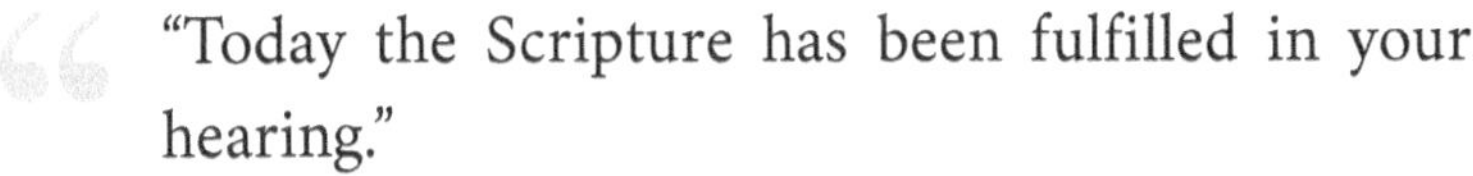

"Today the Scripture has been fulfilled in your hearing."

— LUKE 4:21

"For the prophecy came not in old time by The will of man but holy men of God spake as they were moved by the Holy Ghost."

— 2 PETER 1:21

DAY 4 REMEMBERING ANGEL GABRIEL AND THE ANGELIC HOST

I know that a lot of us don't talk about or think about angels very much these days. I know I don't on a regular basis. The only time I ever really cared or thought about angels was when my parents when I was a child were involved with a church play called "Glory And The Fire" (or "Heavens gates Or Hells Flames") when people would die and see angels in heaven. (They'd have to see if their names were in Lamb's "Book Of Life" to either go to heaven or hell.) Another time I cared or thought about angels was an old classic t.v. show me and my family used to love called "Touched By An Angel" which lasted from 1994 (the year I was born) until 2003 a total of nine years! The show starred Roma Downey who played Monica, (my favorite character!) the late Della Reese who played Tess, (she and Roma Downey carried the show from 1994 until the end 2003) the late John Dye who played Andrew, (He was on season 3 1996 until 2003 season 9) and Valerie Bertenelli who played Gloria (seasons 8 and 9 from 2001-2003) and the show had a total of 211 episodes! (You also can check out "Touched By An Angel" episodes on the Hallmark channel or watch them on youtube and it's a powerful show!) But regardless of whether or not we think about angels, the Bible has alot to say about them. For example the Bible says in Psalm 91:11 "He (God) shall keep His angels in charge of you to keep you in all your ways." God sends angels to protect us which is a good reminder in a dangerous world that we live in!

Simply put, angels surrounded the birth of our Lord. In fact the Bible talks about how an angel appeared to the Virgin Mary, Joseph the carpenter, shepherds, and even the priest Zechariah! (I'll cover those Bible characters more in another chapter) The "main angel" who made appearances was the angel Gabriel! The name Gabriel means "God is my strength" or "a hero of God." Gabriel is also a "high ranking" angel and is known throughout the Bible (in the Old and New Testament) to have given important messages from heaven to God's people. (Michael also is a "high ranking" angel and is known as the warring angel. That's for another topic for another time!) Plus Gabriel and other angels sang praises and glory to God which we know to be "Glory To God in the highest and peace on earth goodwill towards men" Luke 2:14. The angels rejoiced when Jesus was born! And you know what? I'm sure that angels sing in heaven today. I think of Christmas carols such as "Angels We Have Heard On High," "Hark The Herald Angels Sing," and "The Hallelujah Chorus."

I wonder if angels could be singing those songs. Let us rejoice and be thankful that God sent His angels to give messages especially the message about Jesus coming to the world. Let's rejoice today and for all eternity that the promise of that was fulfilled and what a difference it has made in our lives and world!

PRAYER

*"Dear God thank you Lord for promising to send Your
angels to watch over us I pray Lord that You would keep Your
angels over me and my loved ones as we travel in a dangerous
world Thank you Lord for sending Your angels to declare
Christ's arrival and prepared the world for His birth Help me
Lord to continue to rejoice in song for the arrival of Your Son
and declare it to the world I ask this in Jesus name I pray amen"*

SCRIPTURE VERSES

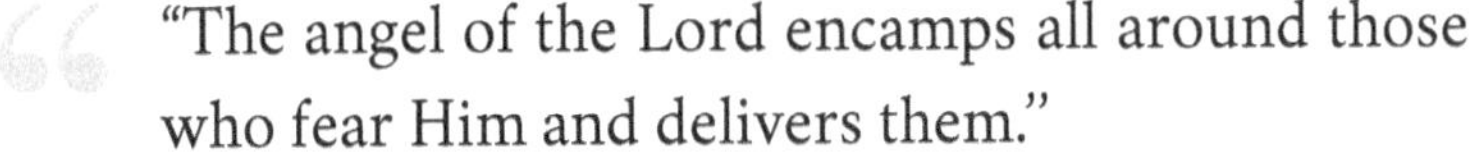

"The angel of the Lord encamps all around those
who fear Him and delivers them."

— PSALM 34:7

"I looked and around the throne saw living crea-
tures and elders, the voice of many angels,
numbering myriads of thousands of voices
'Worthy is the Lamb' that was slain to receive
power, glory, and blessing!"

— REVELATION 5:11-12

DAY 5 REMEMBERING GOD'S PROMISE THE ARRIVAL OF JOHN THE BAPTIST

I know that many of us don't really think about John the Baptist unless we mention him being the "forerunner" for Christ or water baptism. You may also maybe wondering. "What does the coming of John the Baptist have anything to do with Christmas or the Christmas story?" Afterall, he's not in the "Nativity" or his parents! But the birth of John the Baptist is very important because prior to our Lord being revealed, God always sends a message or a messenger to go before Him. That's why we say that John the Baptist was the "forerunner" for Christ because he prepared the way of the Lord. Prior to angel Gabriel appearing to the virgin Mary, angel Gabriel appeared to the priest Zechariah. You can read about it in Luke 1:5-20 when Zechariah was going about his priestly duties and burning incense, (a common practice for priests back then) and the people (including his wife Elizabeth) prayed outside while waiting for him to come out. (The 2006 movie "The Nativity Story" does a very good job portraying that scene as well and suggest you watch it this Christmas!) The Bible says, the angel appeared on the right side of the incense and told him that he and his wife Elizabeth would bear a son and call his name John! The name John means "God is gracious" and man was God gracious to Zechariah and Elizabeth, his wife! The reason is because Elizabeth was barren or what doctors today call "infertile" and especially back then it was a "shameful thing" for a wife to have not conceived.

Sadly though Zechariah did not believe angel Gabriel and was struck mute (unable to speak) for nine months until the baby was born! But thank goodness that Gabriel didn't strike him blind or even worse death due to Zecharaiah's unbelief! (In the Old Testament angels have struck men blind and even killed people for causing trouble!) Also baby John was to be a "Nazarite" (Samson and Samuel were Nazarites as well too) not to drink wine, touch dead things, or cut his hair because Nazarites were to be "consecrated unto the Lord." But also like Samuel and Samson, he was to be a Nazaraite from the moment he was born until the day he died! Baby John was filled with the Holy Ghost in his mother's womb when the virgin Mary visited! After the virgin Mary went home, the Bible says Elizabeth gave birth to baby John in her old age like God promised and the people of Judah rejoiced! Zecharaiah's mouth was loose and praised God and prophesied that his baby boy would prepare the way of the Lord! Now I'm not "equalizing" John the Baptist's birth to Jesus' birth but his birth is important because he had to prepare the way for our Lord to come. Let us be thankful in addition to the birth of Christ thankful God made sure the "forerunner" for Christ also would be born who would grow up to be a Nazarite (not to be confused with "Nazarene" as Christ was) baptize others, and prepare for Christ's arrival!

PRAYER

"Dear God for always preparing a messenger to prepare for Your arrival Thank you Lord for raising up John the Baptist to prepare both Israel and the world for Your Son to come Thank you Lord that John was obedient to Your will and because of him folks have encountered Your Son and lives are changed Thank you Lord in Your name I pray amen."

SCRIPTURE VERSES

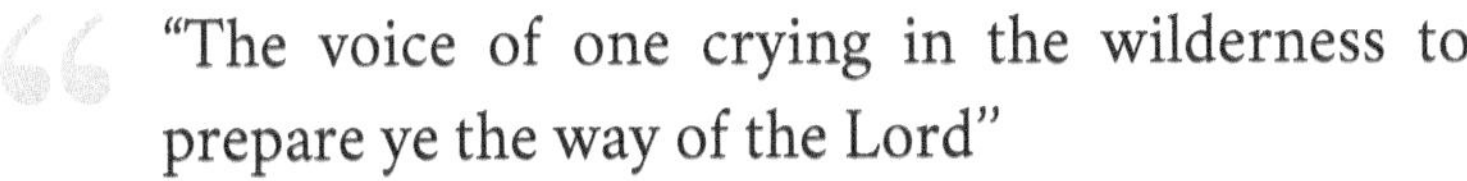

"The voice of one crying in the wilderness to prepare ye the way of the Lord"

— ISAIAH 40:3

"Your wife will conceive and bear you a son and you shall call him John"

— LUKE 1:13

DAY 6 REMEMBERING THE VIRGIN MARY

Oh my goodness. This is such an important chapter y'all. Why? I'm sure most of us know or have heard a thing or two about this lady. Here's some heartbreaking things though. Sadly some people think that the virgin Mary was a "perpetual virgin" (meaning she couldn't have anymore children after Christ's birth) some pray to her, or mistakenly think she's the "mediator between God and man" when the Bible clearly says in 1 Timothy 2:5 that the "mediator is our Lord and Savior Jesus Christ." Some teach falsely that Mary was sinless and some paintings depict her looking "older" when she birthed our Lord! Now I'm not saying that I was taught those things about the blessed virgin Mary but because some "false religions" have taught those things and I want to dispel those myths right now! Beloved, let me tell you something. The virgin Mary was an ordinary person just like you and just like me. She was born with a sin nature like us, she's a "small town girl" (Galilee was a very small town) a teenager, (Likely between the ages 13 to 16 years old. Basically a middle school and high school age kid!) and loved our Lord very much! She likely was a farmer ("The Nativity Story" a film I mentioned earlier does a good job portraying that and most people were farmers back then) and engaged to Joseph the carpenter. (I'll address him in another chapter.)

The angel Gabriel out of nowhere in his "shekinah glory" appeared to the blessed virgin Mary mentioned in Luke 1:26-37 and was told she was chosen by God to be the mother of our Lord and Savior and that His kingdom shall know no end! I can imagine the thoughts going through Mary's head asking how it can be? I also imagine she was worried what her parents, her fiancé Joseph, and religious leaders would have thought of her being pregnant. Being pregnant before the wedding especially back then was what my dad likes to say "taboo" meaning it wasn't an accepted practice. But nevertheless, despite Mary's fear, she said yes to God and Christ would be conceived through the Holy Ghost causing her to get pregnant with Christ. I'm so happy that the blessed virgin Mary said yes despite the challenges she faced. She nearly got in trouble with Joseph her fiancé, (thankfully God intervened) would endure leaving home, facing ridicule from her community, childbearing, and eventually having to leave the country because of Christ's birth! (Herod the Great in Matthew sought to kill Christ after the Magi left. The Magi are in another chapter.) But despite that Mary trusted God and let's be thankful for her courage and obedience and let that motivate us to do the same. What I mean by that is when life throws some challenges after obeying God, like Mary let that make our faith stronger and be a testimony to others on God's faithfulness this Christmas and year around.

PRAYER

"Thank you Lord for choosing the blessed Virgin Mary as Your chosen vessel to bring Your Son Jesus into the world to save us Thank you Lord for giving her the strength to say yes despite the challenges she faced Lord help me to do the same to trust You despite life's challenges from day to day life and perhaps during this Christmas season Help me Lord to be a holy vessel used by You to make a difference to change the world I ask this in Jesus name. I pray amen."

SCRIPTURE VERSES

"The Lord Himself will give you a sign the virgin shall conceive and bear a Son And ye shall call His name Emmanuel."

— ISAIAH 7:14

"For nothing by God shall be impossible."

— LUKE 1:37

DAY 7 REMEMBERING JOSEPH THE CARPENTER/FORGOTTEN HERO

Okay everyone most of us during this time of the year acknowledge and honor the blessed virgin Mary right? We even say Merry Christmas! (ha ha!) But what about Joseph? It seems as though he's a forgotten character or not thought about as much. Yet it seems strange to me that people from "false religions" have their views on Joseph just as they do with his lovely wife the virgin Mary. Someone made up a "false story" that Joseph was "old" when he fell in love with the virgin Mary and that he had a wife and children from his "previous marriage" and married her when she was a teenager! (They are right that Mary was a teenager when they got married but are wrong that he was super old!) Let me stop and say this. No where in Scripture says that Joseph was "previously married!" That's nowhere in the Bible! I do believe that Joseph did get older but as depicted in the movies "Jesus Of Nazareth" (1977) and "The Nativity Story" (2006) the men who played Joseph in those films looked to be in their late twenties early thirties and likely a virgin too! Just as I dispelled myths about the virgin Mary in the previous chapter, I wanted to "dispel" myths about Joseph and say things for what they are. First of all, Joseph was a carpenter by trade, hard worker, and a righteous man. Matthew 1 talks about how his father was Jacob and paternal grandfather was Matthew. He also was born in Bethlehem, grew up in Nazareth, and had a relationship with the Lord.

Now in regards to the blessed virgin Mary, Matthew 1:18 says she was pregnant through the Holy Ghost but Joseph didn't know it. Yet he didn't want to publicly disgrace her and wanted to break the engagement privately. Now why is that significant? Back then if a woman was "sexually immoral," (prostitute or adulterous) the man had the right to take her and the man "in the wrong" and stone them to death! Even the law of Moses permitted that if you can believe that! Joseph could have chosen that but he didn't but then angel Gabriel in a dream showed him that the Child Mary was carrying was conceived by the Holy Ghost and to name Him Jesus because He will save His people from their sins. Joseph got up, married the blessed teenage virgin Mary, and stood up for her. That was also a big deal because I imagine Mary's parents, neighbors, and religious leaders must have thought Joseph was "crazy" because of that but he obeyed anyway. We know that because of the census, he and Mary left Nazareth, and traveled by donkey to Bethlehem! We know that according to Luke 2 there was "no room" in the inn which in our day it would be like a hotel or motel! But nevertheless, they found a stable which likely was either a cave or a barn to stay the night! As we get closer to Christmas let's thank God that Joseph obeyed, stood up for Mary, and helped her bring Christ to the world. It makes me think of our Lord when we were wrong, loved us, forgave us, and restored us despite our brokenness. Joseph and Mary are good examples of saying yes to God regardless of the consequences. Let's pray and ask the Lord to give us courage to do that as well.

PRAYER

"Dear Lord thank you for using Joseph the carpenter to help Mary bring Christ into the world Thank you Lord that Joseph stood up for Mary despite opposition Lord help me stand for You no matter the cost even if it may cost me 'popular opinion' or people's approval Lord help me not only stand for You but stand up for others who can't speak for themselves as well I ask this in Jesus name I pray amen."

SCRIPTURE VERSES

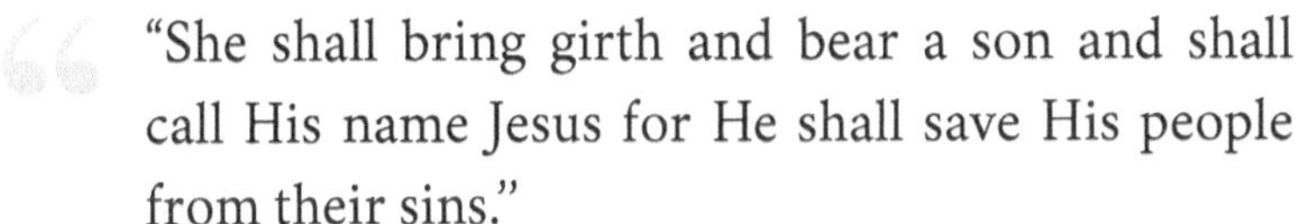

"She shall bring girth and bear a son and shall call His name Jesus for He shall save His people from their sins."

— MATTHEW 1:21

"Unto us a Child is born unto us a Son is given."

— ISAIAH 9:6

DAY 8 REMEMBERING THE SHEPHERDS

I'm sure most of us know this next story by heart. I'm sure even some of you can quote it in your sleep! (Just kidding!) I'm sure you've heard sermons or perhaps watched the movies "Jesus Of Nazareth" (1977) or "The Nativity Story" (2006) or seen plays at churches or theaters depicting the account of the shepherds. Or perhaps as you were driving by, you saw a "Nativity scene" at someone's house or perhaps you may have one in your home or apartment. Simply put, the story of the shepherds is a very "popular" story. But here's the thing though. It's very possible to become "too familiar" with something that you lose the "awe" or "wonder" of it. Imagine this. You're a shepherd and usually at that time the youngest "able bodied" male in the family usually took that job. Shepherds also weren't "highly esteemed" by society back then and a good example of that was David in the Old Testament. Did you know that before David killed Goliath he was a "lowly shepherd boy"? He wasn't esteemed by his family very well but God chose him to be king anyway! Here's another thing. Shepherds had to work "night shift." Why is that? We all know how crazy things happen at night. Shepherds had to protect themselves and sheep from wolves, lions, and bears. Not only that, it's "pitch black" where you can barely see your hand in front of your face! (Aka they didn't have "street lights" back then and I've been up North and it gets dark like that!)

But then out of nowhere angel Gabriel with the "shekinah glory" of God appeared in Luke 2:10-14 and shared the good news. He tells them not to fear that in the city of David a Savior has been born who is Christ the Lord. I'm sure many thoughts were going through their minds about hearing that news. You have to remember the Jews waited a very long time for the Messiah to come. As I mentioned in the previous chapter the prophets predicated a Messiah would come 700 years before it happened! But how many of you know when you wait for something for a long time you somewhat lose hope right? But here's another thing we often overlook. The Jews expected our Lord and Savior to be a "conquering King" and not come as a baby in a manger!

(We know at Christ's Second coming He'll be conquering King and the book of Revelations 19:11-16 talks about that.) But regardless of that, we know the story that the shepherds hurried to the stable or barn and found Mary, Joseph, and baby Jesus. They were filled with joy to the point they told others about the Messiah's birth and Mary kept those things and pondered them in her heart. The good news of Christmas was revealed to "common everyday" people and revealed to the "least of these." Isn't that wonderful? I pray that it is a reminder that God cares about "everyday" people not just "celebrities" and loves to reveal the good news to all who will receive it. Let's be thankful that the gospel message was revealed to us "everyday" people and let's not forget to share it with others too just like the shepherds!

PRAYER

"Dear Lord thank you for revealing the Good news to the shepherds the least of these Thank you Lord for caring about "little ole me" making sure the gospel got to me Lord help me share Your message with others in word or in deed and help me "shine my light" for You to impact others for Your kingdom I ask this in Jesus name I pray amen."

SCRIPTURE VERSES

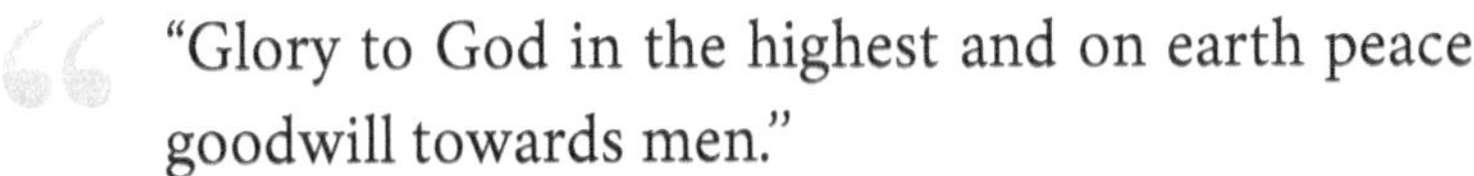

"Glory to God in the highest and on earth peace goodwill towards men."

— LUKE 2:14

"Go into the all the earth and preach the good news to all creation."

— MARK 16:15

DAY 9 REMEMBERING ANNA AND SIMEON

Okay let's be real here. These precious people are not "included" in the "Nativity." I think most of us honestly know very little or anything about Anna the prophetess and Simeon. Honestly I heard very little about this story until I was maybe a teenager and in my early twenties! Regardless of that, this chapter is dedicated to "Christmas in the eyes of Simeon and Anna." Here's another issue I need to address. Alot of people think and it perhaps because of how the "Nativity" is depicted, it depicts that the shepherds and Magi came at the same time. Well let me say when brother Francis created the "Nativity" (I have no issue with brother Francis and I'll honor him in another chapter of this book) that's how he interpreted it so therefore people think the shepherds and Magi came at the same time when that's not true. The shepherds visited Christ at one point and the Magi came later. But right in the "middle" of Christ's birth, Luke 2:21 talks about how Mary and Joseph took baby Jesus to the temple for His "baby dedication" and circumcision. (It was the wish law every firstborn male was to be circumcised and the people were to bring sacrifices as well too. The law of Moses talks a great deal about that.) As Mary and Joseph were going about doing that, the other rest of the story is when Simeon heard the babies cry and went to the temple. Now understand he too had been waiting a long time to see the Messiah and he was old. God promised him he wouldn't "die" until he saw the Christ Child. At that moment, when he saw and held Baby Jesus, he knew it would be time for him to die!

He even went on to say that his "eyes have seen God's salvation" and began to prophesy over Baby Jesus! Wow! Remember in the previous chapter how the shepherds were in "awe" and filled with joy because of Christ's birth? That same joy was upon Simeon an "old prophet." But then he soberly told the virgin Mary that a "sword shall pierce her heart." I'm sure the teenaged blessed virgin Mary didn't understand that at the time but I imagine when the cross happened, I'm sure she remembered 33 years later! As Simeon and Mary and Joseph were saying their "goodbyes" another old prophetess named Anna was there. The Bible says she was in the temple day and night praying, fasting, and seeking the Lord. She got into that lifestyle after the death of her husband. I find that significant because I'm sure most widows would be "bitter" and seeking the last thing on their minds. But not so with Anna. But just like Simeon, she was waiting for the Messiah to come and at the right time, she found Mary and Joseph carrying Baby Jesus. When she saw Baby Jesus she rejoiced, praised the Lord, and prophesied over the

Child and told others He was the promised one of Israel! Wow! Jesus one moment had shepherds and angels rejoicing over His birth and the next moment had two "older prophets" prophesy over His life! Let's rejoice and thank God that He keeps His promise and I pray it's an encouragement to others who may be in their "latter stages of life" that if God kept His promises to Anna and Simeon He can do the same for you who are "older." For those of us like me who may be "younger in age" but we've prayed for something for a while and it hasn't happened yet I pray it's an encouragement to us to believe God for His promises this Christmas and throughout the year.

PRAYER

"Dear Lord, thank you for Your Word. Thank you, Lord, for keeping Your promises to Anna and Simeon, who waited a long time to see the Messiah, but in time, they saw Him Lord. Help me trust in You this Christmas and year around for Your promises. Help me, Lord, be patient and seek You and believe that in Your timing, Your promises will happen. I ask this in Jesus' name: I pray amen."

SCRIPTURE VERSES

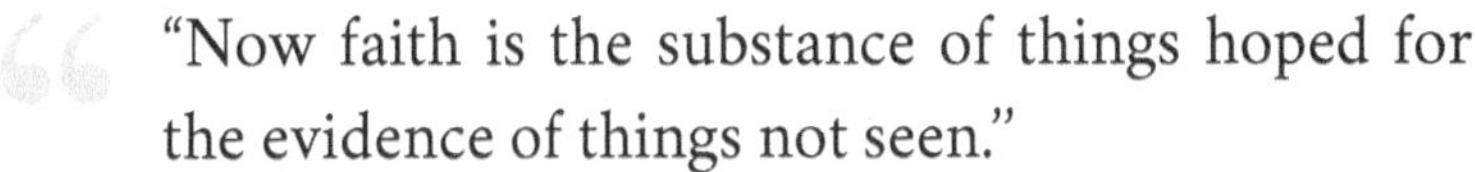

"Now faith is the substance of things hoped for the evidence of things not seen."

— HEBREWS 11:1

"Ye shall call upon me and I will answer If you seek Me with all thine heart ye shall find Me."

— JEREMIAH 29:12-13

DAY 10 THE ADORATION OF THE MAGI

Okay let's get real here. I know that this story is beautiful yet "controversial story." You might be thinking why would I call some "characters" from the "Nativity" controversial? Let me explain. There's a whole lot of "dispute" about the Magi in many, many ways. First there's a "dispute" of how many there were and some think they know the Magi's names. (For instance some belief their names could have been Melchior, Balthazar, and Gasper.) The Bible actually doesn't say how many there were though most people assume it was three and yet there could have been more! Also there's "dispute" on how old Jesus was when the Magi came. Some think that Jesus was still a "baby" while others argue He was a toddler two years old. I worry sometimes that Christians get caught up about these "disputes" and forget the whole point of the story. Here's what you need to remember. Unlike the shepherds and Anna and Simeon the prophet and prophetess, these guys regardless of how many there were weren't Jews! They were Gentiles! Understand back then Gentiles were according to the Jews (not according to God though) "dogs" or "outsiders." Also the Magi were astrologer princes. That means that they studied the stars and planets (you know planets in the solar system like Jupiter, Saturn, Venus, etc.) and were rich men! These guys as some would say were "ahead of their time" especially for knowing/studying the planets even though its "common knowledge" today. But even though they were smart, rich, and were Gentiles, they still were searching for something greater than themselves. Who were they searching for? They were searching for King Jesus!

We know in Matthew 2:2 that the Magi went to Herod the Great and asked who was born the King of the Jews? The Bible says that Herod was disturbed by that and he and religious leaders searched for the Scriptures and read Micah 5:2 that Christ would be born in Bethlehem. Then Herod the Great "tricked" the Magi to search for the Child and come back and worship Him. (Herod the Great was a narcissistic king who killed his wife, sons, and was responsible for the "Massacre of the Innocent" after the Magi returned home.) Well the Magi went on their way to Bethlehem and followed the star to find Christ. I find it very interesting that even creation (the planets Jupiter, Saturn, Venus, and others) were aware of Christ's arrival and helped those weary travelers find our Lord. When they saw Mary, Joseph, and Christ they fell down and worshiped Him and gave Him gifts of Gold, Frankincense, and Myrrh. I love in "The Nativity Story" when the Magi they Christ gifts, they revealed their reasons why. Gold for the King of kings and the book of Revelation 19:11-16 talks about Christ being called that! Frankincense for the Priest of priests and the book of Hebrews 7:24 talks about Christ being our High Priest! Myrrh to honor His sacrifice and we know that John the Baptist prophesied that over Christ in John 1:29 shortly after His water baptism! Also remember most people don't give babies or toddlers gifts like those gifts because the gifts the Magi gave were fit for a king! But we know our Lord was king though He was young! Most people give babies or toddlers clothes or toys. But God our Heavenly Father accepted their offering and it's so beautiful that the story of the Magi is still honored and remembered today. Let us this Christmas time and throughout the year worship our Lord in song like the Magi and give Him gifts of our time, money, and talents as precious gifts to Him.

PRAYER

"Dear Lord thank you for revealing Yourself to us Gentiles Thank you Lord that Your gospel is for everyone Thank you Lord for revealing Yourself to the Magi Help me Lord to worship You in spirit and in truth as Your Word tells us to Lord help my lifestyle and love be a sweet sweet sound in Your ear I ask this in Jesus name I pray amen"

SCRIPTURE VERSES

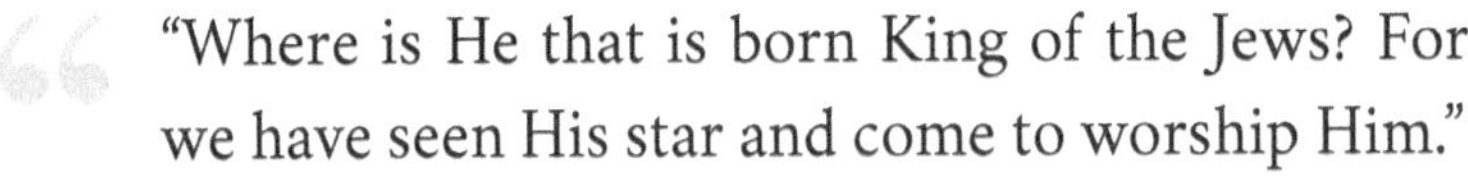

"Where is He that is born King of the Jews? For we have seen His star and come to worship Him."

— MATTHEW 2:2

"God is spirit and those who worship Him must worship Him in spirit and in truth."

— JOHN 4:24

DAY 11 REMEMBERING CHRISTMAS HYMNS

Okay everyone we're "switching gears" a bit. Now we're gonna transition how the Christmas story applies to our day to day lives today. The first ten chapters of the book were looking at Christmas or the good news from the Bible. Now let's apply it to our day to day lives. First let's talk a bit about Christmas hymns. You may ask what is that? You know how there's well known hymns that are sung such as "Amazing Grace," "Nothing But The Blood Of Jesus," "The Solid Rock," "How Great Thou Art", and "A Mighty Fortress Is Our God" are well known hymns right? Well there's hymns we often sing during the Christmas season as well too. Songs such as "Away In A Manger," "O Come All Ye Faithful," "What Child Is This," "Joy To The World." "Hark The Herald Angels Sing" to name a few. Well in this chapter I'll be sharing with you guys the significance of Christmas hymns and how they can help you be in the attitude of worship. For example you know the song "Hark The Herald Angels Sing?" That song was written by the Wesley brothers who heard "church bells ringing" inspired them to write the song? Also did you know that Isaac Watts a Christian and pastor's kid wrote the hymn "Joy To The World?"

The funny thing about "Joy To The World" that song was not "originally" to be a "Christmas hymn." That was actually written for the Second coming of Christ! But after Isaac Watts death, someone used his song for a "Christmas concert" and that's how it got to be a "Christmas carol?" Isn't that something? Now the song "What Child Is This" was written by a Christian man named William Chatterton Dix. What's interesting about him is that he "had a near death experience" from a severe illness but survived. He read the Bible and was inspired by the adoration of the shepherds and Magi and wrote a song to honor that. Now the song "What Child Is This" came from a folk song called "Greensleeves" but Mr Dix changed the "secular lyrics" and turned them to Christian lyrics. What's interesting is last year I wrote blogs about that and I love knowing the "history behind songs" so when I sing them I look at them differently. I know it's possible to get "too familiar" with these songs that they lose meaning. I encourage you and pray that the next time you hear these beloved Christmas hymns that they'll have deeper meaning and encourage you to worship the Lord with all your heart and be thankful that He came.

PRAYER

"Dear Lord, thank you for coming to this world. I pray, Lord, You would help me give You the glory, honor and praise that's due Your name. Help me not take Your presence for granted. Help me to love You in song and with my lifestyle. I ask this in Jesus' name I pray amen."

SCRIPTURE VERSES

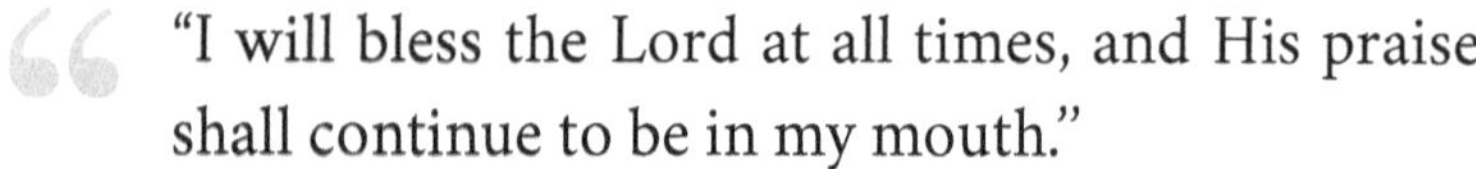 "I will bless the Lord at all times, and His praise shall continue to be in my mouth."

— PSALM 34:1

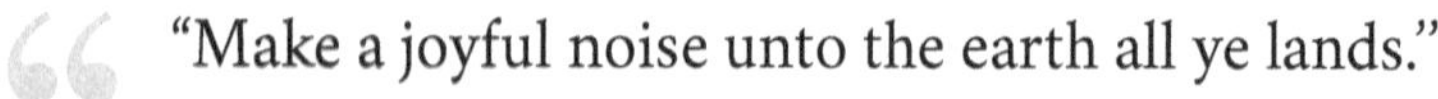 "Make a joyful noise unto the earth all ye lands."

— PSALM 100:1

DAY 12 HISTORY BEHIND CHRISTMAS DECORATIONS

Okay let's be real here. I know alot of us get caught up in "tradition." Let me explain. Have you ever asked yourself why we put up Christmas trees or Christmas lights? Honestly most of us don't even think about that do we? I know I used to not. But I've done a ton of research about the significance and hopefully y'all will do the same too. I remember watching a "Christian Christmas movie" called "The Perfect Gift" which was released in 2009. (I try to watch that every year close to the Christmas season despite the popularity of "Hallmark" Christmas movies!) Some of the information I share here came from that movie in addition to doing research about Christmas decorations. First of all, evergreens. Why is that significant? Evergreens represent everlasting. The Christmas tree could represent Jesus dying on a tree to give us eternal life. Also the Christmas wreath represents the trinity of God. Christmas lights of Christmas candles represent Jesus being the light of the world or represent the angelic host.

Gift giving comes from when the Magi gave our Lord gifts and therefore we give others gifts. Also candy canes are interesting. Turn it right side up is a shepherd's staff and turn it upside down it's a J for Jesus! Plus the little curve represents the beating our Lord took when He was scourged! Wow! Then of course there's putting an angel or star on top of the tree. Of course you put an angel on top of the tree to honor the night that angel Gabriel shared the good news with the shepherds in Bethlehem. If you put a star on the top of the tree it represents the star that guided the Magi from their far away lands (we talked about that in a previous chapter) and how that star led them all the way to Bethlehem until they found our Lord's dwelling place! There's so much spirituality behind Christmas decorations and hope y'all recognize how significant it is and thank our Lord for giving us symbols to remember. Plus the Bible talks about different times that God wanted the Jews to have memorials either by celebrating a holiday or another symbol to remember where they came from. I believe it's important for us Christians to use symbols (especially Christmas symbols) to remember our salvation and what our Lord has done so we don't ever take for granted the Lord's blessings.

PRAYER

"Dear Lord, thank you for the Christmas symbols. Thank you, Lord, how each symbol, in many ways, seeks to honor what You did for us 2,000 years ago. When Christ came the first Christmas night, Lord, make my heart thankful and glad and may I share those traditions with others as the time of honoring Your birth comes closer. I ask this in Jesus' name, I pray, amen."

SCRIPTURE VERSES

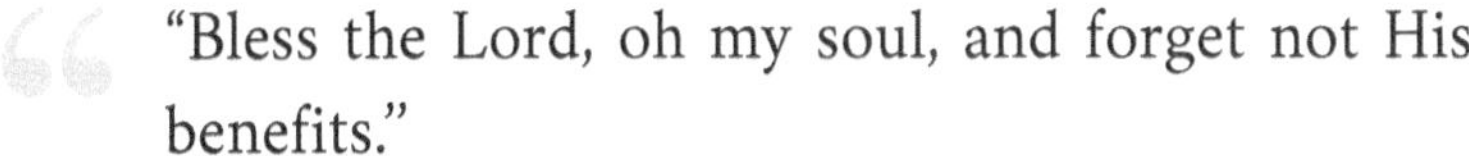

"Bless the Lord, oh my soul, and forget not His benefits."

— PSALM 103:2

"When you have eaten and are satisfied, praise the Lord your God for the good things He's given you. Be careful that you do not forget the Lord your God."

— DEUTERONOMY 8:10,11

DAY 13 BALANCING THE BUSYNESS OF THE SEASON

*L*isten it doesn't take rocket science to know how busy day to day life can be. The busyness of school, work, family, as well as making time for the Lord, and His house. Let's also not forget that those of you who have kids may do extracurricular activities (sports or music) as well as us adults finding balance in doing recreational activities. (I imagine that happens on weekends anyway.) That's enough on a regular day to try adding the holiday season in the mix. Yep, dealing with family coming to town, (out of town company or folks who live nearby) dealing with Christmas parties, (whether hosting them at home, school, or sometimes at work) Christmas plays, (I used to be in one a long time ago) buying Christmas gifts, and so much more! I'm sure some of you may have a headache just looking about all the stuff that must get done before Christmas! But here's the thing. Something that I'm slowly starting to learn is when seasons like that are busy, how important it is to seek God and learn to pace myself the right way. I'm not a complete expert at this but I believe it's important to learn balance during this busy time of the year but also day to day life too.I think about Mary and Martha of Bethany. Most of us I'm sure know the story and know it well. It's mentioned in Luke 10:38-42 Jesus and His disciples were visiting and Mary of Bethany sat at His feet while her sister Martha was busy cooking and cleaning. She got upset and asked our Lord to stop Mary from listening to Him and help her! But our Lord graciously said. "Martha, Martha you are troubled by many things but one thing is needed. Mary has done a better thing and it won't be taken away from her." Remember when Mary and Joseph traveling to Bethlehem in Luke 2:7 looking for a place to stay but the innkeeper had no room for them in the inn? We know that they had to stay in a cave which would be the place our Lord was born in a manger full of hay. Simply put the world was "busy" when Christ arrived as a baby during the first Christmas. Guys it's very obvious that Christmas is a very busy time but will we make room for Christ in our schedule? We know that if we want to spend time with our loved ones we often strive to reprioritize for that to happen. Why don't we do that for our Lord? Friends I believe it's so important in the midst of our day to day lives especially during the holiday season, when we are busy learning to "slow down." Does that mean neglect our responsibilities? No! I'm a part-time college student, own a business, direct an online women's program (you can read the epilogue about my women and kids program) in addition to writing books! But I don't ever neglect my personal time with the

Lord. I believe it's critical to ask the Lord to give you balance during this Christmas season and year around. It's very important ask the Lord what things you need to maybe "pull back on" as well too. What things are an absolute priority and what are some things to put on hold. It's so important to be in good spiritual and mental health during the holidays and year around for ourselves, our loved ones, and our Lord. Let's ask God today to give us balance so we can be productive and live more meaningful lives.

PRAYER

"Dear Lord, help me in the midst of the busyness of the Christmas season and year-round to learn proper balance. Help me not get too busy to spend time with You, and help me include You in my daily schedule. Lord, help me manage my time wisely daily and help Me know how to pace myself. Help me, Lord, also know when to slow down to be with You and prioritize self-care so I can be a better Christian and better for those around me. I ask this in Jesus' name. I pray, amen."

SCRIPTURE VERSES

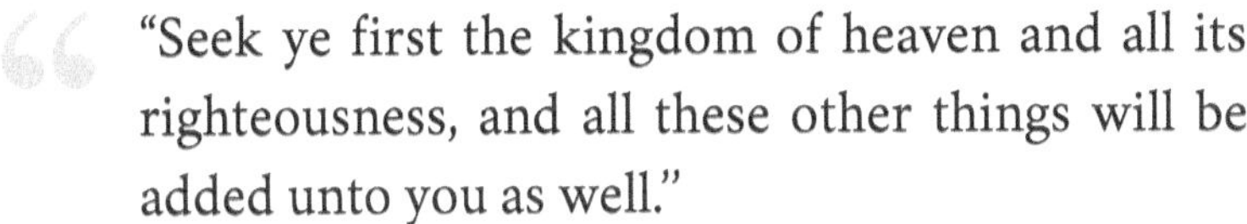

"Seek ye first the kingdom of heaven and all its righteousness, and all these other things will be added unto you as well."

— MATTHEW 6:33

"They that wait on the Lord shall renew their strength They shall mount on wings as eagles They shall run and not be weary They shall walk and not faint."

— ISAIAH 40:31

DAY 14 DEALING WITH HARDSHIPS DURING THE HOLIDAYS

*L*et's be honest here we all know that life can be hard year around right? Everything from job loss, financial troubles, family trauma, loss of loved ones, divorce etc. Some of you may be widowed or perhaps never married in the midst of couples during this time of year. Those things are tough to deal with year round. Just imagine dealing with those things during the holidays? Although it's very well true that Christmas can be the "most wonderful time of the year" but honestly it can also be the most challenging time of the year. I'm sure most of you know that being a Christian doesn't shield us from going through hard times which is the point why I wrote my first book called "Strength For Enduring Adversity." I wrote that book to talk about stuff I've been through various losses and there were seasons when the holidays were tough. I want to address that here in this chapter. Maybe finances are tight for you during the Christmas season and you wonder how you're gonna afford to buy gifts, much less pay your bills. Maybe there's family drama going on or maybe you lost a loved one earlier in the year. Maybe a loved one died sometime ago but the grief still lingers on. If the holiday season is tough for you, know you're not alone. I've been there and I'm sure there's countless others who understand it.Here's another point to remember.

When Christ came the first Christmas 2,000 years ago it wasn't a very happy time. There were political issues (the Roman empire and the brutal Herod the Great) and corruption from spiritual leadership. (Aka we still face challenges in politics today too more than ever!) But that's when God sent His Son to be light in a dark world both naturally and spiritually. I want to encourage you if the holidays are tough for you remember that Jesus is Emmanuel "God is with us" and cleave to Him during the tough times. Also surround yourself with positive people who will love and pray for you during this time. If you also need a moment to process your pain do so and I'd encourage you to go to a Christian counselor too. I'd also encourage you to listen to music that reminds you of Christ's birth but also reminds you that Christ is with you through the hard times. That's something that I had to do in the past and present so that I don't "drown in my sorrows." I'd also urge people if they know someone who's going through a hard time during the holidays don't be too hard on them. Learn to love, listen, care, and most of all pray. As we conclude this chapter hard times can happen year around and the holiday season but remind ourselves that with God we can make it.

PRAYER

"Dear Lord, thank you that You're with me and those around me. If anyone around me is hurting, help me, love and be kind to them. I pray that You would comfort them as well. Lord help me if the holiday season is tough on me, and help me to lean on You during this time. Help me to have a positive attitude and remember that when You came, it was a dark time, too. Use the hard stuff to bring You glory. I ask this in Jesus' name, I pray, amen."

SCRIPTURE VERSES

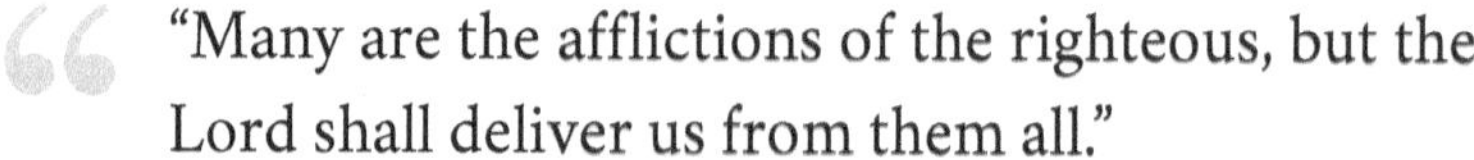

"Many are the afflictions of the righteous, but the Lord shall deliver us from them all."

— PSALM 34:19

"Blessed are those who mourn, for they shall be comforted."

— MATTHEW 5:2

DAY 15 TREASURING LOVED ONES

How many of you know family and friends can be the biggest blessing but also can be the most challenging? I'm sure all of us know a relative or two that have what I call a very "dynamic Lord have mercy personality." (What I mean in a nice way is that they're not the easiest to get along with.) How many of you also know that holidays can unfortunately bring out some "unhealthy disputes" to cause even more trauma? Friends I know this all too well and I'm sure some of you know this too. Maybe there's a relative who likes to argue politics, (I don't tolerate that at all. No way Jose!) or undealt with issues between spouses or siblings. Maybe there's disputes about who's house to go to or maybe a relative who's kind of "the black sheep" and some relatives don't like them as much or at all. People may wonder if "the black sheep" is worth inviting over at all. It's so important to learn how to handle those issues the right way and most of all pray for those issues as well. Also if need be to go to counseling feel free to do so as well too. Here's another thing: what about people who aren't here during the holiday season? That's something that I briefly addressed in chapter one: reasons why people could be away from away. I know that times like this can be hard too and bring out difficult emotions.

I know from experience that loved ones living or those who have died can bring out some feelings of sadness. In times like that pray to God and ask for help during these times. Perhaps try to find common ground and learn when to at times "put things to the side" and remember the most important things in life. Maybe it could work through conflict the right way and also discerning when's the best time to talk and when to be quiet. The most important thing for us all to remember that the holiday season is about Christ and that should be the main focus. Whether folks in your family or friends are saved or not I think there needs to come a point to keep main stuff (especially about Christ) front and center. If your loved one is deceased, perhaps find a way to pay tribute to them. What was their favorite song, dish, movie, or joke? If they were a Christian, what was their favorite Bible verse or Christmas carol? It won't take all the bad feelings go away but perhaps doing those things can help. Let's pray that as we meet with loved ones that God will be honored and that unity can occur.

PRAYER

"Dear Lord, I pray You will help me get along with loved ones during this holiday season and year-round. If there's tension and strife, help that to dissipate in Jesus' name, Lord, to comfort me and comfort others who lost a loved one. Most of all, help us find a way to still have joy and find ways to honor You and them to make the season joyful. I ask this in Jesus' name; I pray amen."

SCRIPTURE VERSES

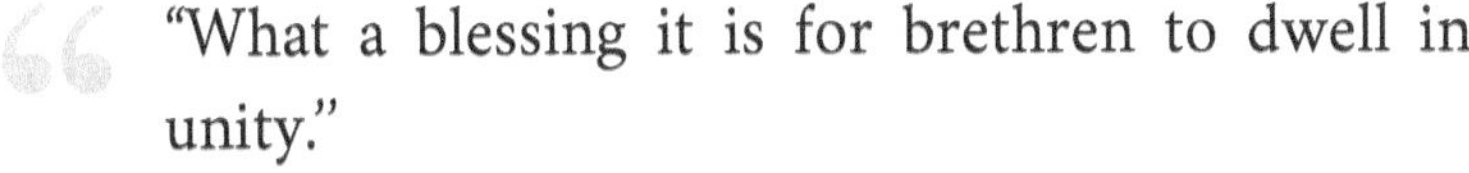

"What a blessing it is for brethren to dwell in unity."

— PSALM 133:1

"This is My commandment that Ye love one another as I have loved you."

— JOHN 15:12

DAY 16 LEARNING TO BE JOYFUL

How many of you know how beautiful yet challenging our emotions can be? I know all too well from experience. It's often said that women tend to be more "emotional" than men. Whether that theory is true or not, emotions are powerful. Even God has feelings. Did you know that? In fact the Bible talks about different times in the Old and New Testament how God was happy about something and other times He was deeply grieved over things. Just as we human beings have things that grieve our spirit, God is the same way too. But in this chapter we're focusing on being joyful. God is joyful and wants us to be as well too. Let me also clarify. Does having joy mean we're happy all the time or that we're "ignorant" of hard stuff? No! But I heard someone describe joy as "either content or joy is relational." We can be joyful not because of our circumstances but because of someone we're in a relationship with. Christian if you may have lost your joy or life seems to be draining ask the Lord to give it to you. I know I've had to do alot especially the past few years after enduring many losses that I had to ask God to restore that to me. Change may not occur overnight but I promise you that can happen.

Let me also ask you this. I What are things that bring joy to God's heart? I think most of us who have known the Lord for quite awhile have an idea what things make Him delighted. Well when we spend time with Him, praise Him, be in His house, and help others. He also delights when we walk in love too. The Bible says in Psalm 37:4 "Delight ourselves in Him and He'll give us the desires of our hearts." What are things that make you smile? Maybe you like a certain song, like to hang out with friends, go shopping, or a favorite movie. Here's another important question to ask. What are some things that drain you? What I mean is things that drain us often "suck the joy" out of us. Could it be toxic relationships,(romantic, friendships, family members etc) toxic work environment, social media, bad music, or things like that that are dragging you down emotionally? That's something that I'm learning to be aware of the older I get is to be aware of things, people, or environments that drag one down. I'm more prayerful and cautious about it and walk away if need be from stuff like that. I pray as Christmas approaches that we're joyful about what Christ has done and if you lack joy pray that God gives it to you.

PRAYER

"Dear Lord, I pray, Lord, that You would give me joy, Lord; I pray that You would help me be aware of the things that suck the joy of my life. Whether it's people, things, or environments, help me be aware and walk away from that stuff, Lord; help me be positive and not pessimistic. Help me to remember the good things You've done for me in the past and present. I ask this in Jesus name I pray amen."

SCRIPTURE VERSES

 "The joy of the Lord is my strength."

— NEHEMIAH 8:10

"Weeping may endure for a night, but joy cometh in the morning."

— PSALM 30:5

Most of us know that the Christmas season is a season of giving right? I know you might be thinking. Shouldn't we be giving year around? Of course we should! I think about Malachi 3:8 tells Christians to give tithes to the storehouse so God's people should give to the Lord's work. That's one example of that. Another point about Christmas is we often know John 3:16 that says "For God so loved the world that He gave His only begotten Son. Whosoever believes in Him shall not perish but have everlasting life." Simply put you guys, God is a giver not a taker! How much more should we His people be? Remember when I said in a previous chapter where the tradition of gift giving came from the Magi? I know alot of us love to give Christmas gifts to our loved ones and friends but what about being a blessing to people in need during this time of year? I think about when I was a teenager (probably in the year 2008 which was also within the recession hit) when my dad got hurt at work (he tore his acl) caused him to be out of work for a short time. It was a challenging time because my mom was a house-wife/homeschool mom (I was probably fourteen and my siblings were twelve and eight years old) putting them on a one budgeted income. But you know what? The Lord provided and my dad had surgery and was able to go back to work but it still was a tough time financially for a good while.

But God sent a wonderful Christian family to give us tons of Christmas gifts that year and that will be a Christmas I will always remember and treasure. It's not the "gifts" that mattered, it was the "love" behind it that mattered. As I also mentioned in a previous chapter, Christmas can be a hard time for people. One way I mentioned some people may or may not be able to afford stuff during the Christmas season. Perhaps you know someone in that position. Could you consider financially helping them or buying Christmas gifts for them especially for children whose loved ones may not be able to afford to buy them gifts? Perhaps they may not be able to afford a "traditional" Thanksgiving or Christmas meal, perhaps inviting them to your house or serving at a "soup kitchen" a holiday meal for them. Perhaps visiting the elderly in a "nursing home" or prison, maybe singing Christmas carols to them or giving them Christmas cards. Perhaps doing something kind for veterans or baking cookies for the home-less? As I continue to get older I pray to be able to help others more during this time of the year. Let's pray that we in the body of Christ put our love to action helping others "not to be seen" but doing it to show Christ's love. As we meet people's "practical needs" let's do that with the intention to meet their spiritual needs as well too.

PRAYER

"Dear Lord, I thank You for all the times You met my needs. Lord, help me and my loved ones be on the lookout for people in need. Lord, give me Your heart for the poor as well as the lost. Help me and my loved ones be generous and not selfish. Help me to do it for Your glory, and I do it for me to shine Your love. I ask this in Jesus' name, I pray, Amen."

SCRIPTURE VERSES

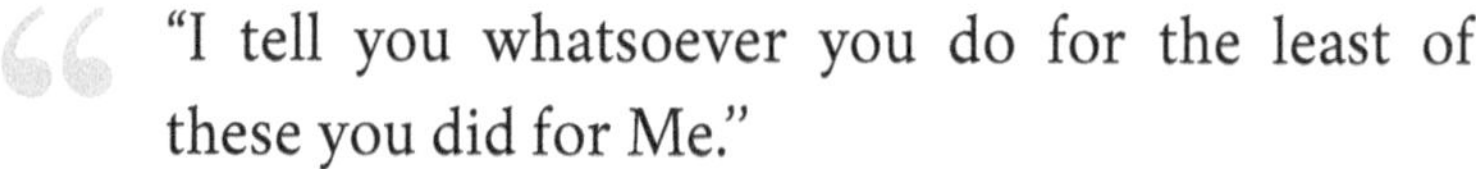

"I tell you whatsoever you do for the least of these you did for Me."

— MATTHEW 25:40

"He that lends to the poor lends to the Lord."

— PROVERBS 19:17

DAY 18 HONORING SAINT NICK

Okay this chapter I know is an interesting chapter. I know some of you maybe thinking. What in the world does Saint Nick have to do with Christmas? Here's the thing Saint Nick has celebrated on December 6th since the 1000s until now! Here's the thing about this man. He was born in Asia Minor born in 270 AD and died in 343 AD and died about the age of 73 years old. He thankfully was born to wealthy Christian parents and likely got saved at a young age. But it was a tough time for Christians he got persecuted and even imprisoned for a time. But thanks to Constantine the Great (the first Roman leader who converted to Christianity) released him and was able to live as a Christian freely. But that's not the main thing he was known for. He was known for helping countless people in need. In fact at one point he gave to a poor father so his daughters wouldn't go into slavery! Have you ever heard the term "secret santa"? Not that I believe in "Santa Claus" but a "secret santa" is when someone gives a lavish gift or a simple gift but doesn't want to say who gave it? In fact I can remember back in 2020 that I was at a Christmas party at a youth group where we ate great food and it was time for a gift exchange. I remember particularly being given a winter coat but the gift bag said "Disciple of God" on it. They did it because they didn't want me to know where it came from! That's something I will never forget.

Well Saint Nick was alot like that. He would give to people in "secret" and not want them to know who gave it. Simply put Saint Nick was a giver! But he's called "saint" because he was a Christian! Here's another interesting fact about Saint Nick. Did you know that we get "Santa Clause" from Saint Nick? We know Santa Claus (well it's a fictitious story) how he comes down the tree to deliver gifts to kids? That idea came from Saint Nick people! If you recall in the previous chapter I talked about the importance of helping people in need and being givers? I also emphasized how God is a giver because He first gave His Son Jesus Christ? Well I believe that honoring Saint Nick's legacy goes along very well with remembering people in need. I also love to read inspiring stories like this and I don't know about you, it sometimes motivates me to do something positive to make a difference in the world. So the next time you think of or celebrate Saint Nick, (the holiday is December 6th) I hope and pray that you remember "the real meaning" of his story. I pray most of all it will compel us to help people in need both naturally and spiritually and motivate us to live a legacy of love.

PRAYER

"Dear Lord, thank you for using different people throughout history who touched the world for the better, especially Saint Nick Lord. Forgive me for selfishness and, being caught up in my life and family, and I forget others in need. I pray, Lord, You'd give me your eyes and help me be Your hands and feet in a world in need, Father. Help me go and touch the world through the power of Your love. I ask this in Jesus' name, I pray, amen."

SCRIPTURE VERSES

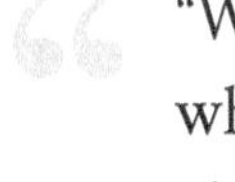

"When you give, don't let your left hand know what your right hand is doing so that you are giving may be in secret. What your Father who sees what is done in secret will reward you."

— MATTHEW 6:3,4

"It is more blessed to give than to receive."

— ACTS 20:35

DAY 19 REMEMBERING BROTHER FRANCIS

Okay everyone. I know you maybe thinking? Who in the world is brother Francis? Francis Of Asisi was a wonderful man Christian who was born in 1181 and died in 1226 about 44 years old. You may wonder. What in the world does he have to do with Christmas and how is he relevant today? Well friends in this chapter I'm gonna reveal the answer why he's significant and how God used this fellow to transform what we know today for the Christmas season. He was a guy who at one time was from a wealthy family and a wealthy noble and was known as Francis of Asisi. But he later became sick and reevaluated his life. Then he often spent time by himself and one day he saw a "vision from the Lord" and urged him to "repair His Church!" (Side note if you think seeing "visions from Jesus" is weird that's happening in alot of Muslim nations with them seeing Jesus in dreams and getting saved! I think I'd just throw that out there!) Well brother Francis did so and unfortunately it would cause persecution from his family and would have to leave them behind to continue in his mission, and grow in his Christian walk. One day he visited the holy land which also changed his life.

He realized many people who were poor couldn't read or write the Bible so he decided to do what was the first "live Nativity" and would have people act out the Christmas story! (Side note: people who were poor back then didn't have the "luxury" of reading and writing and the poor have much to be thankful that that's not so today!) He did what is called today "illustrated messages" people seeing the Bible in action! He also would do that during a Christmas Eve service as well too. Overtime "live Nativities" would evolve into statues, Nativity plays, and Nativity movies! (Side note brother Francis may have been ignorant of the actual timeline of the shepherds and Magi's arrival because they didn't arrive at the same time, it's still something to be honored though!) Also brother Francis wrote many Christmas carols too such as "O Come All Ye Faithful" and "Silent Night!" Isn't that something? So many Christmas carols sung today and Nativity scenes we see are because of this man's brother Francis! I'm sure he had no idea that doing that would cause the Christmas story to spread for the next several hundred years to what we have today. Let us thank God for brother Francis for his dedication to serving the Lord and getting the Christmas story spread and let us continue to do the same as well too.

PRAYER

"Dear Lord, thank you for Brother Francis for being obedient to Your will no matter what the cost. Thank you that he spread Your gospel near and wide. Lord, help me to do the same, to say yes to Your will and the way no matter the cost, and to make Your gospel known to all. I ask this in Jesus' name, I pray, amen."

SCRIPTURE VERSES

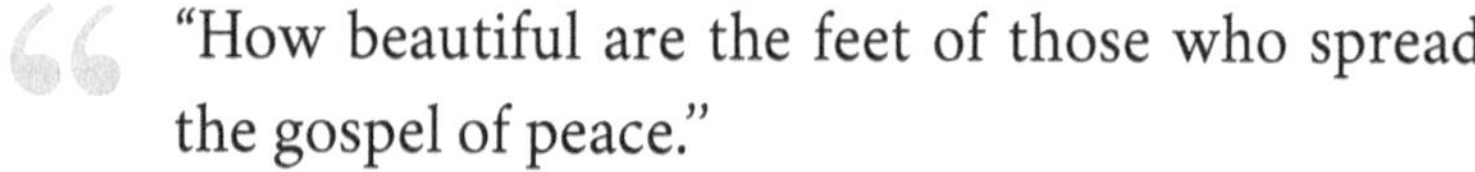

"How beautiful are the feet of those who spread the gospel of peace."

— ISAIAH 52:7

"The harvest is plentiful, but the workers are few. Therefore pray earnestly that the Lord of the harvest send out laborers to His harvest field."

— MATTHEW 9:35-36

DAY 20 RECOGNIZING CHRIST'S PRESENCE IN OUR LIVES''

ell friends, we have finally come to the end of the book. Even though it may be the last chapter of the book, there's still so much to live and learn. I hope you have learned and enjoyed much by reading each chapter and finding ways to apply lessons learned. Here's the thing, friends. Christmas is all about Christ! In fact if you take the word Christmas and subtract the "mas" from "Christmas" you'll get the word Christ! Yes indeed. Christmas is all about Christ coming down from heaven to earth and how His presence changed the world! As we read in previous chapters how His birth impacted the "Nativity characters" such as the virgin Mary, Joseph, shepherds, and the Magi. The good news or the Christmas story impacted them and their lives were never the same. God enabled the Christmas story to be recorded in Matthew and Luke Scripture verses I'm sure that many of us know by heart.I want you to know that the Christmas story impacts lives today. Perhaps you may have given your life to the Lord during this time of year or got saved at a different part during the year.

Anybody can know the story of Christ or Christmas. It's not until when the person encounters the "Christ of Christmas" that it changes lives. That occurs at salvation. But it's also important to continue knowing and serving Christ. It's critically important to receive the baptism in the Holy Ghost mentioned in Acts 1:8 when Christ promises the "dunima power" where we get the English word dynomite. It's when we encounter the Holy Spirit (evidence of speaking in tongues) that we get to experience God's presence in a deep way on earth and lie for Him effectively. It never ceases that when I pray or I listen to worship music like songs like "O Come All Ye Faithful" or "O Holy Night" I sense the Lord's presence. It's my prayer that you and your loved ones experience Christ's presence in a deeper way this Christmas season. Perhaps you're reading this and don't know Christ as Lord and Savior or maybe you're a prodigal. Maybe you once knew the Lord but walked away. I'd encourage you to give your life to Christ or come to Him and if you know Hm already get to know Him better. Let's celebrate not only Christ's presence that came to the world during the Christmas story and how it impacts lives today which is the greatest news the world could ever know.

PRAYER

"Dear Lord, I come to You in Jesus' name thank you for the difference You've made in my life. Thank you for the difference You made 2,000 years ago. Help me, Lord, to treasure Your presence this Christmas and the year around. Help me to love You more and more each day. I ask this. In Jesus' name, I pray amen."

SCRIPTURE VERSES

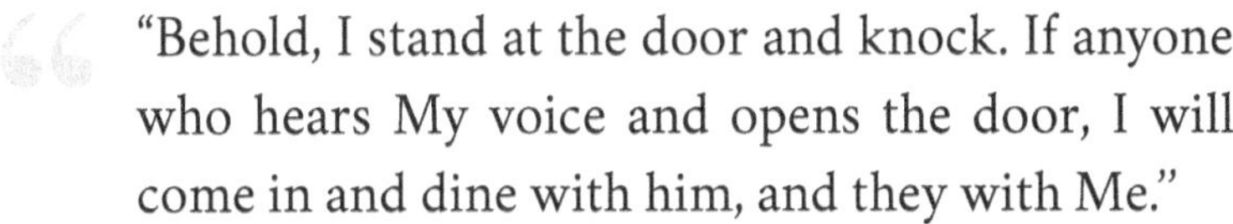

"Behold, I stand at the door and knock. If anyone who hears My voice and opens the door, I will come in and dine with him, and they with Me."

— REVELATION 3:20

"In the presence of the Lord, there is fullness of joy."

— PSALM 16:11

Perhaps you've never given your life to Christ or are backslidden. I want you to pray this prayer with which goes like this;

"Dear Heavenly Father I come to You in Jesus name Thank you Father for sending Your Son Jesus as a baby in manger that came the first Christmas night to be light in darkness to grow up one day to die on the cross for me and rise again I admit I have sinned and fallen short of Your glory Please forgive me of my sins and wash and cleanse me with Your blood I accept You Jesus into my heart this Christmas season and help me to live for You throughout the year baptize me in the Holy Ghost evidence speaking in tongues so I can live for You effectively, feel Your presence, and touch the world I ask this in Jesus name I pray amen."

If you prayed that prayer and meant it the Bible says in 2 Corinthians 5:17 "If anyone is in Christ he or she is a new creature. Old things have passed away and all things have become new." I'd encourage you to read and apply the Bible daily starting with the Christmas story. I'd encourage you to pray everyday and spend quality time with the Lord and get into a Bible believing Spirit filled church. I'm sure there are many wonderful churches in your area. If you don't feel comfortable in a "traditional church setting" especially if you're a lady you can check out my online ministry called "Women's Warriors Academy" where we meet most Sunday nights for Bible study (I cancel if it's a major holiday or some other major reason) and meet for prayer Tuesday nights. One way or another a Christian needs "community" to continue to grow as a Christian. God bless each and everyone of you guys and pray that you all have a Merry blessed Christmas and Happy New Year!

EPILOGUE

Ever been overwhelmed by the storms of life? Have you endured multiple hardships in one year that left you breathless, helpless, and struggling to move forward? Sommer Kelly knows those challenges all too well and has shared many of the hardships she went through in her first book called "Strength For Enduring Adversity" that came out earlier this year. In that book she addresses how life was before the fall, how to cleave to God during brokenness, knowing what stages of grief one is in, and how God can use our trials for His glory. She also shares how people in the Bible went through things and shared some personal things of her life as well that were painful such as job loss, loss of loved ones, and broken dreams. If you or someone who knows is going through a storm, Sommer prays that this book will help encourage others to know God is with them and can turn their broken pieces into something beautiful. You can find it on her website or find it on Amazon. Go and pick up your copy today!

Are you also looking for an online kids community? Sommer has worked tirelessly to "improve" the "virtual experience" and has started an online kid/teen program called "Young Lives Art Center." The purpose of those online programs is to meet women and children where they are related to biblical truth, interact, do fun things, and interact while online. "Young Lives Art Center" specializes in book club music, art class, Spanish, and many other fun activities while in the comfort of their home. They usually meet on Zoom, Google Duo, or Google Meet and have "age appropriate" activities for preschoolers and older (age groups are separate) whenever is convenient for the parents schedule. It's Sommer's prayer that children be impacted by the gospel of Christ and if you want more information about her kids program go to the younglivesartcenteronline.com or call her (414) 640-1380 to connect with her personally and meet the online community!

Are you a Christian lady looking to connect with other godly women in a more small and intimate way? Well that's what "Womens Warriors Academy" is all about. "Women's Warriors Academy" is a virtual women's ministry that meets online Sunday nights at 7 P.M. (they cancel unless it's a holiday or another major reason) and meet for virtual prayer meetings Tuesday nights at 7 P.M. (unless they cancel for an extreme reason or change to a different day.) For Bible study they dive into topics that are related to the challenges of this world with a biblical perspective and for prayer meetings they pray about individual needs as well as pray for America. They also have an online store where one can purchase various Christian items and ya'll can check out my women's website called womenswarriorsacademy.com to check out those things. 75

ACKNOWLEDGMENTS

First and foremost I'd like to thank my Lord the Father, Son, and Holy Spirit for everything. Thank you Father for adopting me as Your child, thank you Jesus for coming to earth 2,000 plus years ago as a Baby in a manger to grow up to die on the cross for our sins and rise again to make us right with the Father. Thank you Holy Spirit for helping me live the Christian life, knowing the Bible better, and enabling me to write this book along with my previous one. I'm forever thankful for You Lord for all You are and what You've done for me. Thankful to my parents for instilling me a strong Christian foundation and for instilling me hard work. To my siblings and brother-in-law for making my life interesting and making the holidays more fun. To my pastors and folks at "New Life Assembly Of God" Church I'm so thankful to have known y'all the past four years. I'm thankful that you guys supported me with my previous book and trust that y'all will continue to do so. To the pastors that have blessed me over the years thank you so much. I honor and bless y'all in the name of the Lord. (You know who you are.) I'd like to thank Joy Anderson, Lina Munoz, and all my Preschool All Stars family. I'm thankful that you ladies continue to walk this journey to inspire me to be a better entrepreneur.. Thank you ladies for your continued friendship, encouragement, and prayers as I seek to be the entrepreneur God has called me to be. To my "Women's Warriors Academy" family I love doing online ministry with y'all especially Bible study Sunday nights (most nights that is) and virtual prayer meetings Tuesday nights. (most nights) You ladies have been one of my biggest cheerleaders that have meant the world to me. To my clients for my virtual businesses. I love having y'all as clients and thankful for supporting my God given vision. For my MATC (Milwaukee Area technical College) professors, I'm thankful to continue to learn from you guys. It's been a long journey but I know that in time I look forward to college graduation and when it does, I'll never forget y'all. To my close friends, intercessors, and my therapist, I'm so thankful to have y'all in my life. You guys know "the real me" and I'm thankful for your loyalty which is a rare precious gift to have. To my music teacher Lena Vinz, thank you for motivating me to be a better musician. To 123 websites company, thank you guys so much for your encouragement and working with me on both my women's website and my kids website. I'm thankful for you guys' tireless dedication and I'm thankful to be your client.To the Spines publishing company, I'm so thankful to walk this journey again with you guys. You guys walked me through the publishing of my first book and you guys are here again for round 2 with the second one! Words can't express how truly thankful I am that you guys in my opinion are "super-heroes" for seeing potential in me as an author, something I've dreamed of since I was a little girl. I believe the best is yet to come with more books for the future. To my beautiful, loving, God-fearing, prayer warrior, funny, and wise godfather thank you so much! I'm so thankful for our friendship, words of wisdom, and motivating me to keep growing in the Lord. We may live far away from each other, you never cease to check on me, pray for me, share encouraging words, and believe in me despite you and I's busy schedules. God, you, and my therapist have walked me through some difficult times but I'm better because of it. And lastly to the readers. Thank you all so much for purchasing this book. It means the world to me that of all the books you could have read you chose to read my book. Thank you all so much for your prayers, support, and encouragement. I pray that this book encourages y'all to keep Christ in the center of Christmas as well as in your day to day life. This is my "second book" by God's grace and looking forward to sharing more with y'all in the future. God bless!